ADAM HAMILTON

SIMON PETER

FLAWED BUT FAITHFUL DISCIPLE

CHILDREN'S LEADER GUIDE
BY SALLY HOELSCHER

Abingdon Press / Nashville

Simon Peter
Flawed but Faithful Disciple
Children's Leader Guide

978-1-5018-4612-0

18 19 20 21 22 23 24 25 26 27 — 10 9 8 7 6 5 4 3 2 1
MANUFACTURED IN THE UNITED STATES OF AMERICA

Contents

To the Leader

This children's leader guide is designed for use with Adam Hamilton's book *Simon Peter: Flawed but Faithful Disciple*. This guide includes six lessons that take a look at Simon Peter's life and ministry. Children will hear about Peter's life and explore learnings from Peter's story that may be applied to their own lives.

The lessons in this guide, designed for children in kindergarten through the 6th grade, are presented in a large group/small group format. Children begin with time spent at activity centers, followed by time together as a large group. Children end the lesson in small groups determined by age. Each lesson plan contains the following sections:

Focus for the Teacher

The information in this section will provide you with background information about the week's lesson. Use this section for your own study as you prepare.

Explore Interest Groups

Ideas for a variety of activity centers will be found in this section. These activities will prepare the children to hear the Bible story. Allow the children to choose one or more of the activities that interest them. Occasionally there will be an activity that is recommended for all children, usually because it relates directly to a later activity. When this is the case, it will be noted in the sidebar notes.

Large Group

The children will come together as a large group to hear the Scripture and story for the week. This section begins with a transition activity, followed by the story and a Bible verse activity. A worship time concludes the large group time.

Small Groups

Children are divided into age-level groups for small group time. Depending on the size of your class, you may need to have more than one group for each age level. It is recommended that each small group contain no more than ten children.

Younger Children
The activities in this section are designed for children in grades K-2.

Older Children
The activities in this section are designed for children in grades 3-6.

Reproducible Pages

At the end of each lesson are reproducible pages, to be photocopied and handed out for all the children to use during that lesson's activities.

Schedule

Many churches have weeknight programs that include an evening meal; an intergenerational gathering time; and classes for children, youth, and adults. The following schedule illustrates one way to organize a weeknight program.

5:30	Meal
6:00	Intergenerational gathering introducing weekly themes and places for the lesson. This time may include presentations, skits, music, and opening or closing prayers.
6:15–7:30	Classes for children, youth, and adults.

Churches may want to do this study as a Sunday school program. This setting would be similar to the weeknight setting. The following schedule takes into account a shorter class time, which is the norm for Sunday morning programs.

10 minutes	Intergenerational gathering
45 minutes	Classes for children, youth, and adults

Choose a schedule that works best for your congregation and its Christian education programs.

Blessings to you and the children as you explore the life and ministry of Simon Peter!

1. Jesus Calls Peter to Follow Him

Objectives	Bible Story
The children will: • hear the story of Jesus calling Peter to be a disciple. • discover that Jesus called Peter to fish for people. • explore what it means for them to follow Jesus.	Jesus Calls Peter to Follow Him Luke 5:1-11 **Bible Verse** "Don't be afraid. From now on, you will be fishing for people." (Luke 5:10b)

Focus for the Teacher

Today we begin a six-week study of one of Jesus' disciples: Simon Peter, often simply called Peter. Over the next six weeks, children will hear stories about Peter. Children will explore ways to apply learnings from Peter's life to their own lives.

Today's Bible story begins in Luke chapter 5 with Jesus standing beside Lake Gennesaret, also known as the Sea of Galilee, where he sees two fishing boats. Fish was a dietary staple in first-century Palestine. Consumed more than any other meat, fish was eaten fresh, processed, salted, dried, or pickled. Therefore, fishing was an important industry on the Sea of Galilee. Jesus, however, doesn't want to fish; he wants to use a boat to sit in while he teaches the crowd on shore. He climbs into one of the boats and asks its owner, Simon Peter, to row him out from the shore.

Although this story is usually referred to as Jesus calling the disciples or Jesus calling the fishermen, it is primarily the call of Peter. Peter is the only disciple introduced prior to this scene, when Jesus heals his mother-in-law.

> Jesus calls us as we are to do God's work.

Peter is the only one to speak to Jesus, and Jesus' commission is directed at Peter. James and John, the sons of Zebedee, are mentioned almost as an afterthought in verse 10 as Peter's partners. We know, however, that James and John did follow Jesus also.

Peter had done nothing special to warrant being called by Jesus. He was not called because of his qualifications. Rather, the interaction began because Jesus wanted to use Peter's boat. Peter had something Jesus needed. This is reassuring to those of us who might wonder whether we are qualified to follow Jesus. Jesus calls us as we are to do God's work. God finds ways to use the skills we have—and sometimes our stuff. Jesus called Peter for a specific commission. He doesn't simply say, "follow me," as he does in some other call stories. He tells Peter that he will be "fishing for people." Peter's mission is evangelistic in nature. Having been called, he is now to go out and gather people into God's kingdom. Like Peter, we are also called to follow Jesus and given the task of fishing for people.

Explore Interest Groups

Be sure that adult leaders are waiting when the first child arrives. Greet and welcome each child. Get the children involved in an activity that interests them and introduces the theme for the day's activities.

Fishnet Tag

- Choose four children to be the fishnet. Have the four children hold hands with each other.

- **Say:** These four children are the fishnet, and the rest of you are fish. If you are caught by the fishnet, then you will become part of the net.

- Let the children play the game until most of the fish have been caught. Choose four different children to be the fishnet and play again.

Prepare
✓ Identify a large open area free of obstacles to play the game.

Beaded Fish

- Give each child a chenille stem.

- Have each child fold the chenille stem in half to form a V shape.

- Have each child thread an equal number of beads onto each half of the chenille stem, leaving approximately 2 inches of chenille stem empty on each side.

- Have each child twist the two ends of the chenille stem around each other one time just above the last beads.

- Have each child shape the beaded portion into a fish shape.

- Have each child add beads to both ends of the chenille stem, leaving enough chenille stem empty to bend over the last bead.

- Have each child spread the beaded ends into a V shape.

- **Say:** The fish shape is a symbol of Christianity. Some of Jesus' first followers were fishermen

Prepare
✓ Provide chenille stems, pony beads, and bowls.
✓ Place the pony beads in the bowls and spread the bowls out across the work area.

Prepare

✓ Make copies of **Reproducible 1a: Fishing at the Time Jesus Lived.**

✓ Provide pencils.

✓ *Answers*: fresh, processed, salted, dried, pickled, carp, catfish, circular, parachute, bottom, clean, remove, repair

Fishing in Bible Times

- **Say:** Today's Bible story is about Jesus calling a fisherman to be one of his disciples. At the time Jesus lived fishing was an important industry because fish was eaten more than any other meat. Fishing was hard work and took a lot of time.

- **Ask:** Have you ever been fishing? Did you use a fishing pole?

- Allow children an opportunity to share their fishing experiences.

- **Say:** Peter, Andrew, James, and John used nets to catch fish. Let's learn more about fishing at the time Jesus lived.

- Give each child a copy of **Reproducible 1a: Fishing at the Time Jesus Lived.**

- Encourage the children to work individually or in pairs to figure out the coded words.

- Read the information aloud.

Large Group

Bring all the children together to experience the Bible story. Use a bell to alert the children to the large group time.

Fishing for People

- Have the children stand on the opposite side of the room from you.

- Invite two children to come over to your side of the room.

- Tell the children that each of them should go back to the other side of the room and invite two more children to join you. (There will now be a total of six children.)

- Continue sending the children over to each invite two more children until all of the children are with you.

- Say: Although you may not have realized it, you have been fishing for people. That's what our Bible story is about today.

Simon Peter's Story

- **Say:** Today we are beginning a six-week study about one of Jesus' disciples whose name was Simon Peter.

- **Ask:** Will we find Simon Peter's story in the Old Testament or the New Testament? *(New Testament)*

- **Say:** The New Testament tells us about Jesus' life and ministry and is where we find stories about what Jesus' followers did after Jesus' resurrection. Today's story is from the Gospel of Luke. We are going to hear the story as if Peter were telling it to us.

- Invite your recruited volunteer to tell the story from **Reproducible 1b: Jesus Calls Peter to Be His Disciple**.

- Thank your volunteer for telling the story.

- **Ask:** What did Jesus mean when he told Peter he would be fishing for people? *(Peter would be telling people about Jesus and inviting them to follow Jesus too.)*

- **Say:** Jesus called Peter to be one of his disciples. As Jesus' disciple, Peter learned how to tell people about God's love and teach people how God wants them to live

Prepare

✓ Provide copies of **Reproducible 1b: Jesus Calls Peter to Be His Disciple.**

✓ Recruit a volunteer to come and read the story of Peter each week during this study

Prepare

✓ Write the week's Bible verse on a markerboard or a piece of mural paper and place it where it can easily be seen: "Don't be afraid. From now on, you will be fishing for people." (Luke 5:10b)

Bible Verse in Three Parts

- Show the children the Bible verse.

- **Say:** Today's Bible verse is something Jesus said to Peter.

- Encourage the children to read the verse with you.

- Divide the class into three groups.

- **Say:** Now we are going to divide our verse into three parts. The first part will be, "Don't be afraid." The second part will be, "From now on," And the third part will be, "you will be fishing for people." The first group I point to will say the first part of the verse, the second group I point to will say the second part of the verse, and the third group I point to will say the last part of the verse. Pay attention so you know what to say when I point to your group.

- Point to each group several times and encourage the children to say the Bible verse.

Prepare

✓ At the top of a large sheet of posterboard, use a marker to write the following words: Like Peter, we can...

✓ Display the poster where children will be able to see it and where it can remain throughout the study.

Learning from Simon Peter

- **Say:** Today we heard the story of Jesus calling Simon Peter to follow him. Jesus calls us to follow him too. Like Peter, we can decide to follow Jesus.

- Show the children the poster you started.

- **Say:** As we hear Peter's stories over the next weeks, we will use this poster to remember what we learn from Peter.

- Write the following words under the heading on the poster: Decide to follow Jesus.

- **Ask:** What does it mean to follow Jesus? (*To follow his example, to live as he taught*)

- **Say:** As followers of Jesus, we follow Jesus' example about how to live and how to treat other people.

- **Pray:** *God, here we are, ready to follow Jesus' example and teachings. Help us to do your work in the world. Amen.*

- Dismiss children to their small groups.

Small Groups

Divide the children into small groups. You may organize the groups around age levels or around readers and nonreaders. Keep the groups small, with a maximum of ten children in each group. You may need to have more than one group of each age level.

Young Children

- Have the children sit in a circle. Place the objects you have collected in the center of the circle.

- **Say:** Jesus told Peter that he would be fishing for people. Since we are Jesus' followers, we are fishers of people too.

- **Ask:** What does it mean for us to be fishers of people? *(We can tell people about God's love and invite people to follow Jesus.)*

- **Say:** Like Peter, we can invite people to learn more about Jesus. That makes us fishers of people. Anytime we are following Jesus' example about how to live we are fishing for people.

- Invite a child to choose one of the objects.

- **Ask:** How could we use this object to fish for people?

- Allow children an opportunity to share their ideas.

- Continue inviting children to choose objects and brainstorm about how they could be used to fish for people until each child has had an opportunity to choose something.

- **Say:** Of course, we don't really need any special equipment to fish for people.

- **Ask:** What are some ways we can fish for people that don't require any additional equipment? *(There are many examples, such as smiling at someone, offering a hug, sharing a laugh, listening, and so forth.)*

- Allow children an opportunity to share their ideas.

- **Say:** This week, look for ways to fish for people.

- **Pray:** *God, help us to look for ways we can share your love with other people. Thank you for loving us. Amen.*

Prepare

✓ Provide a variety of items useful in ministry such as a Bible, soup pot, cell phone, shovel, coat, offering plate, musical instrument, bandages, cup, envelope, crayons, and so forth.

Prepare

✓ *Optional*: Provide a tackle box to show the children.

Older Children

- **Say:** Jesus told Peter that he would be fishing for people. Since we are Jesus' followers, we are fishers of people too.

- **Ask:** What did Jesus mean when he told Peter he would fish for people? *(He would invite people to follow Jesus.)* What does it mean for us to be fishers of people? *(We can invite people to follow Jesus and tell people about God's love.)*

- **Say:** Like the disciples, we can invite people to learn more about Jesus. That makes us fishers of people.

- **Ask:** Have you ever heard the expression, "actions speak louder than words"? What does that expression mean?

- **Say:** We can tell people about God's love and invite them to follow Jesus, but if we are not living as Jesus taught us to live, our words are not going to have much effect.

- **Ask:** How would we fish for people with our actions?

- Allow children an opportunity to share their ideas.

- **Say:** Anytime we are following Jesus' example about how to live we are fishing for people with our actions.

- If you have a tackle box, show it to the children.

- **Ask:** Do any of you have a tackle box that you use to go fishing? Or do you know someone who has a tackle box? What kind of things would you find in a tackle box?

- **Say:** People who like to fish often have a special box that they use to keep bait and other things needed while fishing.

- **Say:** We have talked about the kinds of actions that help us fish for people. Imagine that you are putting together a tackle box of actions that are useful for fishing for people.

- **Ask:** What kind of actions would we not want in our fishing for people tackle box?

- **Say:** Remember to look for opportunities to fish for people this week.

- **Pray:** *God, we want to follow Jesus and fish for people. Help us to live as Jesus teaches us to live and look for ways to do your work. Thank you for loving us. Amen.*

Fishing at the Time Jesus Lived

Decode the words in parentheses. Hint: A=1, B=2, C=3, etc.

At the time Jesus lived, fishing was an important industry on the Sea of

Galilee. Fish was eaten more than any other meat. It was eaten

____ ____ ____ ____ ____ , ____ ____ ____ ____ ____ ____ ____ ____ ____ ,
6 18 5 19 8   16 18 15 3 5 19 19 5 4

____ ____ ____ ____ ____ ____ , ____ ____ ____ ____ ____ , or
19 1 12 20 5 4   4 18 9 5 4

____ ____ ____ ____ ____ ____ ____ . The most common kinds
16 9 3 11 12 5 4

of fish in the Sea of Galilee were ____ ____ ____ ____ and
3 1 18 16

____ ____ ____ ____ ____ ____ ____ .
3 1 20 6 9 19 8

Much of the fishing at the time was done using a cast net. A cast net was a

____ ____ ____ ____ ____ ____ ____ ____ net with weights around the
3 9 18 3 21 12 1 18

bottom edge. A skilled fisherman could throw it out in such a way that it

opened completely and sank to the bottom of the water like a

____ ____ ____ ____ ____ ____ ____ ____ ____ , trapping fish beneath it.
16 1 18 1 3 8 21 20 5

The fisherman would dive into the water and carefully pull the

____ ____ ____ ____ ____ ____ of the net together and collect the
2   15   20   20   15   13

fish. Interesting side note: Since the use of this type of net required

the fisherman to jump in the water frequently, he usually fished

without any clothes on!

After they finished a round of fishing, fishermen had to

____ ____ ____ ____ ____ their nets. They had to
3   12   5   1   14

____ ____ ____ ____ ____ ____ all fish from the mesh and
18   5   13   15   22   5

____ ____ ____ ____ ____ ____ any holes.
18   5   16   1   9   18

Jesus Calls Peter to Follow Him

Based on Luke 5:1-11

Hi! My name is Simon Peter. I was one of Jesus' disciples. Sometimes people call me Simon—that was my given name. Sometimes people call me Peter. Do you have a nickname that your friends sometimes use? Peter was a name that Jesus gave me. Sometimes people use both of my names and call me Simon Peter.

Today I want to tell you about the day Jesus called me to follow him and be his disciple. I had been fishing all night on the Sea of Galilee with my brother, Andrew, and our friends James and John. We did most of our fishing at night so the fish wouldn't see the nets. That night had been frustrating because we hadn't caught any fish. After we finished a night of fishing, we had to take care of our nets by cleaning and repairing them. This is what we were doing that day when Jesus came to the Sea of Galilee. People followed Jesus to hear him teach, and that day there was a large crowd listening to Jesus.

Jesus was standing on the shore teaching the people, but then he noticed our boats sitting by the lake. Jesus got into my boat, and then he asked me to row him out a little distance from the shore. I did what Jesus asked. Jesus sat in my boat and taught the crowd of people. From the boat, Jesus was able to teach the crowd and people were able to see and hear him. Jesus told the people about God's love.

After Jesus finished speaking to the crowds, he said to me, "Row out farther, into the deep water, and drop your nets for a catch."

I explained to Jesus that we had been fishing all night and we hadn't caught any fish. But for some reason, I followed his instructions anyway. I rowed the boat into deeper water. And when I dropped the net, I caught so many fish that I had to call James and John to come and help me pull up the nets. Our boats were so full of fish that they began to sink. It was amazing. I knew right then that Jesus was a special person.

Jesus said an interesting thing to me. He said, "Don't be afraid. From now on, you will be fishing for people."

After we brought the boats to shore, I followed Jesus and became one of his disciples. My brother, Andrew, and my friends James and John became disciples of Jesus too. Just like Jesus had said, we learned to fish for people.

2. Jesus and Peter Walk on Water

Objectives

The children will:

- hear the story of Jesus walking on the water.
- discover that Jesus was with the disciples when they were frightened.
- explore what it means to know God is with them all the time.

Bible Story

Jesus and Peter Walk on Water
Matthew 14:22-34

Bible Verse

Just then Jesus spoke to them, "Be encouraged! It's me. Don't be afraid."

(Matthew 14:27)

Focus for the Teacher

As we continue our study of Simon Peter, this week we look at the story of Jesus walking on the water and inviting Peter to join him. In biblical tradition, water is often seen as representing chaos. The only one who has power over this chaos is God. In the Old Testament, God is described as controlling the water during creation. During the Exodus of the Israelites from Egypt, God's power over water is displayed in the parting of the Red Sea. When Jesus walks across the water to reach his disciples who are in a boat, it is a sign that he has God's power over the water, proving that he is God's son.

> God repeatedly reminds us not to be afraid.

In Matthew's Gospel, the story of Jesus walking on the Sea of Galilee immediately follows Jesus' feeding of the multitudes with five loaves of bread and two fish. After Jesus finished teaching, he makes his disciples get in the boat and set sail without him while he dismisses the crowds. After Jesus had sent the crowds away, he went up on a mountain by himself to pray.

Meanwhile, strong winds have come up on the lake and the boat the disciples are in is being battered by the waves. Storms are common on the Sea of Galilee because it is surrounded on nearly every side by mountains. While the disciples are in the boat surrounded by waves, Jesus walks across the water to them. The disciples at first think he is a ghost. Jesus calls out to them, "Be encouraged! It's me. Don't be afraid." God repeatedly reminds us not to be afraid. "Don't be afraid" is the most frequently spoken phrase from God to humans in Scripture.

Even after Jesus calls out to the disciples and reassures them that it is he, Peter demands proof. "If it is you, order me to come to you." Jesus issues an invitation to Peter to come to him. Peter gets out of the boat and begins to walk on the water also. But as Peter starts across the water he becomes frightened and begins to sink. Peter was a faithful disciple, but as this story shows, sometimes it was a struggle for him to have faith. We can be reassured by the knowledge that even a faithful disciple such as Peter had moments of doubt. Jesus was there for Peter when Peter became frightened and began to sink. We can trust that Jesus will be with us, too, no matter where we are or what we are feeling.

Simon Peter: Children's Leader Guide

Explore Interest Groups

Be sure that adult leaders are waiting when the first child arrives. Greet and welcome each child. Get the children involved in an activity that interests them and introduces the theme for the day's activities.

"God Is with Us" Mural

- Encourage the children to look through the magazines and cut out the indicated letters, cutting out a lot of each letter. The letters may be any size, color, or style.

- **Say:** We are going to use these letters to spell out the phrase, "God is with us."

- Invite children to use the cut-out letters to spell the phrase, "God is with us," gluing the letters in order on the mural paper.

- Have children keep working to spell the phrase as many times as they can with the letters they have cut out.

- **Say:** God is always with us, no matter where we are or what we are doing.

Prepare

- ✓ Cut a large piece of mural paper or provide a large piece of posterboard.

- ✓ Provide glue, scissors, and old magazines that may be cut up.

- ✓ Look through the magazines and remove any pages that contain inappropriate pictures or articles.

- ✓ Write the following letters on a piece of paper: D G H I O S T U W. Write the phrase, "God is with us." on a separate piece of paper.

Walking on Cornstarch Water

- Show the children the cornstarch and water.

- **Say:** We are going to have some science fun today.

- Pour the cornstarch into the large bowl.

- Slowly add water to the cornstarch, stirring it as you go with a spoon or with your hands. There is no set cornstarch to water ratio, but it will take approximately one cup of water for two cups of cornstarch. Add water and mix until the mixture is viscous. It will seem to alternate between being a solid and a liquid.

- Pour the mixture into a shallow container or cookie sheet.

- Encourage the children to experiment with the mixture that will seem to be part solid and part liquid.

- Have the children notice how they can slide their fingers across the top of the mixture, but if they hold their fingers still their fingers will sink.

Prepare

- ✓ Provide a 16-ounce box of cornstarch, pitcher of water, large bowl, shallow container or cookie sheet and spoons.

- ✓ *Note:* When you are finished with this experiment, place the mixture in a plastic bag and throw it in the trash. Do not put it down the drain.

- ✓ *Tip:* If you have a large class, divide children into small groups and make several batches of cornstarch and water to allow everyone to have a turn experimenting with the mixture.

- **Say:** If you made enough cornstarch and water mixture to fill a swimming pool, you would be able to walk across it if you walked quickly. If you stood still you would sink.

- **Ask:** Would you be able to do that in a swimming pool filled with water?

- **Say:** Of course not. We cannot walk on water, but in our Bible story today we will hear about a time Jesus and Peter walked on water.

Prepare

✓ Form a circle of chairs facing inward, using one less chair than the number of children in your class.

What Can You Do?

- Choose one child to stand in the center of the circle of chairs, and have the rest of the children sit in the chairs.

- **Ask:** Can any of you walk on water?

- **Say:** Of course not! But each of you has many abilities and there are many things that you can do.

- Explain the following rules to the children:

- Everyone in the chairs will ask the person in the center, "Can you walk on water?"

- The person in the center will reply by saying, "No, but" and then telling something they can do, such as "No, but I can play the trumpet," or "No, but I can play soccer," or "No, but I can read."

- Every person in the circle for whom that statement applies must get up and find a new seat while the person in the middle tries to get a seat also. Your new seat may not be right next to your old seat.

- The person left standing remains in the middle to be asked, "Can you walk on water?"

- At any time if the person in the middle answers the question "Can you walk on water?" with "No, but I can trust in God," then everyone must get up and move.

- Encourage the children to play the game.

- **Say:** In our Bible story today we will hear about a time Jesus walked on water.

Large Group

Bring all the children together to experience the Bible story. Use a bell to alert the children to the large group time.

Row Your Boat Across the Lake

- Encourage children to follow your instructions as you give directions.

- **Say:** Imagine that the floor of our room is a big lake. Look, there are some boats on the lake. Everyone pretend to climb into a boat. Have a seat and pick up your oars. Let's row across to the other side of the lake. Dip your oars into the water and begin rowing. Row. Row. Row. Work together with the others in your boat to keep rowing. Make sure that everyone isn't rowing on the same side of the boat or you'll go in circles. The wind is picking up and starting to create waves that are rocking the boat. Stop rowing and pretend that your boat is rocking in the water. It's getting windier and the boat is rocking harder. Finally, the wind has slowed down and the water is calm. Let's row a little bit farther. We've reached the shore. Pretend to place your oars in the bottom of the boat and climb out of the boat.

Simon Peter's Story

- **Say:** Last week we heard the story of Jesus calling Simon Peter to be a disciple.

- **Ask:** Do you remember what Peter's job was before he became Jesus' disciple? *(Fisherman)*

- **Say:** Today we are going to hear another story from Peter.

- Invite your recruited volunteer to tell the story from **Reproducible 2a: Jesus Walks on Water**.

- Thank your volunteer for telling the story.

- **Ask:** Can ordinary people walk on water? *(No)*

- **Say:** God has the power over creation, including water. Because Jesus is God's Son, he could walk on water.

- **Ask:** Why do you think Peter and the other disciples were afraid when they saw Jesus walking on water? *(You don't see people walk on water.)* What do you think Peter was afraid of when he realized he was walking on water? *(That he would sink.)*

- **Say:** When the disciples saw Jesus walking on the water, they knew he was God's Son.

Prepare

✓ Provide copies of **Reproducible 2a: Jesus Walks on Water**.

✓ Recruit a volunteer to come and read the story of Peter each week during this study.

✓ Write the week's Bible verse on a markerboard or a piece of mural paper and place it where it can easily be seen: "Just then Jesus spoke to them, 'Be encouraged! It's me. Don't be afraid.'" (Matthew 14:27)

Control the Volume of the Bible Verse

- Show the children the Bible verse.

- Encourage the children to read the verse with you.

- **Ask:** Which three words of the Bible verse were also in last week's Bible verse? *(Don't be afraid.)*

- **Say:** For two weeks we have heard Jesus reassuring Peter and telling him to not be afraid.

- **Ask:** Do you remember why Jesus had to reassure Peter and the other disciples in the Bible story we heard today? *(There was a storm and the disciples thought Jesus was a ghost when they saw him walking on the water toward them.)*

- **Say:** Now let's pretend that I am a volume control slider. We will sign and say the verse together three more times. When I am standing over here (move all the way to your right side) the volume needs to be very soft. As I walk across the room, the volume increases and when I am standing over here (move all the way to your left side) the volume is very loud.

- Encourage the children to say the verse with you three more times as you control the volume with your position.

Prepare

✓ You will need the poster started last week.

Learning from Simon Peter

- Show the children the poster about learning from Peter.

- **Say:** Last week we began hearing stories about Simon Peter. We learned that like Peter, we can follow Jesus.

- **Ask:** What have you done this week to follow Jesus? How have you followed Jesus' example and teachings this week?

- Allow children an opportunity to share.

- Add the following words to the poster: Trust in God's presence.

- **Say:** Jesus reminded Peter and the other disciples not to be afraid because he was with them. Like Peter, we can learn to trust that God is always with us. Wherever we go and whatever we are doing, God is with us.

- **Pray:** *God, thank you for your loving presence with us. Help us to remember that we can count on you to be with us when things are going well in our lives and when life is challenging. Amen.*

- Dismiss children to their small groups.

Small Groups

Divide the children into small groups. You may organize the groups around age levels or around readers and nonreaders. Keep the groups small, with a maximum of ten children in each group. You may need to have more than one group of each age level.

Younger and Older Children

- Today we heard Peter's story about walking on the water with Jesus. Let's see what we can remember about the story.

- Encourage the children to work together to retell the story.

- **Say:** Jesus reminded Peter and the other disciples not to be afraid and to trust in God's presence. We know God is always with us.

- **Ask:** Is there anywhere you can go that God will not be with you? Does the fact that God is with us mean life will always be easy? *(No)*

- **Say:** Sometimes everything in our life is going well. Sometimes life is challenging. We face difficult situations. God is with us no matter what.

- **Ask:** How does it make you feel to know God is always with you?

- **Give the children time to respond.**

- **Say:** We are going to spend some time remembering God is with us regardless of how we are feeling or what is happening in our lives. I am going to have you close your eyes while I read some statements. After each statement I will invite you to take a deep breath and then let it out.

- Invite the children to find a comfortable sitting position and to close their eyes.

- Read the following statements slowly and calmly:
  o Silently remember a time you were very happy. God is with you when you are happy.
  o *Take a deep breath…and let it out.*
  o Remember a time you were excited. God is with you when you are excited.
  o *Take a deep breath…and let it out.*
  o Remember a time you were hurt. God is with you when you hurt.
  o *Take a deep breath…and let it out.*
  o Remember a time you were angry. God is with you when you are angry.
  o *Take a deep breath…and let it out.*

Prepare

✓ *Note:* Although all children are doing the same activities in their small groups this week, the level of discussion will vary according to the age of children in each group.

- o Remember a time you were sad. God is with you when you are sad.
- o *Take a deep breath…and let it out.*
- o Remember a time you felt loved. God is with you and loves you all the time.
- o *Take a deep breath…and let it out.*

- Invite the children to open their eyes.

- **Say:** No matter what is happening in our lives and what we are feeling, we remember that, like Peter, we can trust God to be with us.

- **Pray:** *God who was with Peter and is still with us, thank you for loving us. Thank you for Peter's stories that teach us about you. Amen.*

Jesus Walks on Water
Based on Matthew 14:22-34

Hello! Simon Peter here again. Last week I told you about Jesus using my boat and calling me to fish for people. Today I want to tell you another story about Jesus. This story also involves my boat.

One day I was with Jesus and the other disciples. We were next to a big lake called the Sea of Galilee. Jesus had been teaching people all day, and it was getting late. Jesus told us to get in the boat and go on across the lake while he dismissed the crowd and took some time to pray. The other disciples and I did what Jesus asked us to do.

During the night as we were crossing the lake, strong winds came up on the lake and made huge waves. Our boat was far from shore and the waves were beating against the boat. It was pretty scary! As we looked out across the water, we saw a figure coming toward us, walking right across the water. We thought it was a ghost!

Then the figure called out to us, "Be encouraged! It's me. Don't be afraid."

I thought it sounded like Jesus' voice, but how could Jesus be walking on the water? I said, "Lord, if it's really you, order me to come to you."

It really was Jesus, and he invited me to come to him. I got out of the boat and started walking across the water to meet Jesus. Yes, I was really walking on the water! But then I became frightened because I shouldn't have been able to walk on the water, and I began to sink. "Help me!" I cried. Jesus was right there and reached out his hand to grab me. He got us both in the boat.

The other disciples and I knew that Jesus had to be God's son. No one else would have been able to walk on the water. When Jesus got in the boat, the wind calmed down and we rowed to shore.

I try to have faith and trust in God's presence with me, but sometimes, like that night, I forget and become frightened. Jesus reminded me that I can trust God to be with me.

3. Peter the Rock

Objectives

The children will:

- hear the story of Peter recognizing that Jesus is the Messiah.

- discover that Jesus gave Simon the name of Peter, meaning "rock."

- explore ways to acknowledge Jesus in their own lives.

• Bible Story

Peter Recognizes Jesus as the Messiah
Matthew 16:13-23

Bible Verse

Simon Peter said, "You are the Christ, the Son of the Living God."

(Matthew 16:16)

Focus for the Teacher

This week's story about Peter focuses on identity. The first part of the story addresses Jesus' identity, both from the viewpoint of Peter and the other disciples and from those outside of the circle of twelve. Then Jesus addresses Simon Peter about who Peter is and his role in growing the church.

"Who do people say I am?" Jesus first asks the disciples what other people are saying about him. "John the Baptist, Elijah, Jeremiah"—all of the answers given are people who have died or, in Elijah's case, been taken up to heaven. These answers indicate that although people do not realize Jesus is God's son, they have noticed he is special and not of this world. Jesus poses this question not because he needed to know who people said he was, but to serve as a contrast to his next question to the disciples.

"And what about you? Who do you say that I am?" Jesus' true identity is not new to the disciples at this point. They had earlier declared, "You must be God's Son!" after witnessing Jesus walk on water. Jesus asks the question here to highlight that he is building a new community

> Who do you say that I am?

of those who recognize him as God's Son. Though the question was asked of the disciples collectively, Simon Peter, who often served as spokesperson, was the one to answer. "You are Christ, the Son of the living God."

Following Simon Peter's declaration, Jesus blesses him with the words, "Happy are you, Simon son of Jonah." Then Jesus gave Simon a new name. Jesus gave Simon the Aramaic name, Cephas, meaning "rock." In Greek, the name translates to Peter. Jesus then gives Peter a commission, "I'll build my church on this rock." Jesus had plans for Peter. Before Jesus bestowed the nickname of "rock" on Simon Peter, there are no documented instances of anyone using this name in Aramaic or Greek. That Peter is now a common name illustrates the influence of Jesus' nickname for Simon. Jesus tells Peter he will be the foundation of Christ's church. Although Peter is the cornerstone, Jesus is the builder of this new community of believers.

Explore Interest Groups

Be sure that adult leaders are waiting when the first child arrives. Greet and welcome each child. Get the children involved in an activity that interests them and introduces the theme for the day's activities.

Decorate a Rock

- Give each child a paper plate.

- Have each child write his or her name on the plate.

- **Say:** I am going to put a hot rock on your paper plate. Do not touch the rock. If you need to move the rock, do so by moving the paper plate.

- Place a hot rock on each child's paper plate.

- Show the children how to use the crayons to decorate their rocks. When the crayon comes in contact with the hot rock, the crayon will begin to melt onto the rock.

- Encourage children to use crayons to decorate their rocks.

- **Say:** We have been learning about Simon Peter for several weeks. The name Peter means "rock."

- Let the rocks cool on the paper plates until the end of class.

Prepare

✓ Provide rocks, crayons, paper plates, baking sheets, and oven mitts.

✓ *Note*: You will need one rock for each child. Rocks that are fist-sized or larger work well.

✓ *Tip:* Most children will be able to remember to only touch the plate and not the rock. Have oven mitts available for children who might have difficulty remembering not to touch the rock.

✓ Place rocks on a baking sheet in a 300-degree oven for at least ten minutes. The rocks can stay in the oven until you are ready to do the activity.

Prepare

✓ Provide large rocks (fist-sized or larger), paper sacks, paper, straws, tape, string, paper clips, and craft sticks.

✓ In each paper sack place one rock and a variety of other potential building materials such as paper, straws, tape, string, paper clips, and craft sticks. Prepare one sack for each group of children; making sure each sack has the same contents.

Prepare

✓ Provide a rock small enough for children to hide in their hands, but large enough not to be easily lost.

Build a Church

- Divide the class into groups of three or four children each.

- Give each group of children a paper sack.

- **Say:** As a group, I would like you to use the items in the sack I have given you and build a church.

- Encourage the children to work together to build their churches.

- After a set amount of time, have the children admire all of the churches.

- Ask each group about how they used the rock in their building: Did they use the rock as a foundation? Why or why not? If they did not use the rock as a foundation, why did they make that choice? Did that present any challenges? If they did not use the rock at all, why did they make that choice?

- **Say:** Today we will hear Simon Peter's story about Jesus giving him the nickname "rock" and telling him he would build his church on him.

Who Is the Rock?

- Have the children stand in a circle.

- Show the children the rock.

- **Say:** We are going to play a game of hiding and keeping track of the rock.

- Choose one child to be the Rock and one child to be the Searcher.

- Have the Rock and the Searcher stand in the center of the circle.

- Give the rock to the child chosen to be the Rock and have them hold it in cupped hands, hiding it from view.

- Instruct the remaining children to hold their hands in front of them, cupping them as if they were holding something.

- **Say:** The Rock is going to go around the entire circle and pretend to pass the rock to each person. One time they will actually pass the rock but will continue on until they have visited each person. The Searcher must watch carefully to see who has the rock.

- Have the Rock go around the circle, visiting each child and passing the rock to one of the children.

- **Say:** Now the Searcher will try to guess who the identity of the new Rock. If you are asked, "Are you the Rock?" you must open your hands.

- Give the Searcher up to three tries to find the new Rock.

- When the new Rock has been identified or after three attempts, choose a new Searcher and play the game again.

Simon Peter: Children's Leader Guide

Large Group

Bring all the children together to experience the Bible story. Use a bell to alert the children to the large group time.

Rock On

- Have the children stand up.

- **Say:** Pretend you are sitting in a rocking chair and rocking.

- Encourage children to rock back and forth as if they were sitting in a rocking chair.

- **Say:** Now pretend you are in a boat and you are rocking the boat.

- Encourage children to rock side to side as if they were rocking a boat.

- **Say:** Now pretend you are listening to rock music.

- Encourage children to dance to the pretend music.

- **Say:** Now pretend you are a rock on the ground, maybe a tiny pebble or a huge boulder.

- Encourage children to squat down, curl up and hold very still.

- **Say:** It is the last rock that we will hear Jesus refer to in the story we hear from Peter today.

Simon Peter's Story

- **Say:** Today we are going to hear another story from Simon Peter.

- Invite your recruited volunteer to tell the story from **Reproducible 3a: Peter Recognizes Jesus as the Messiah.**

- Thank your volunteer for telling the story.

- **Ask:** What do you think Jesus meant by saying he would build his church on Peter?

- **Say:** Jesus wanted to make sure that Peter and the other disciples understood who he was. This was important because Jesus knew Peter would play an important role in starting the church.

Prepare

✓ Provide copies of **Reproducible 3a: Peter Recognizes Jesus as the Messiah.**

✓ Recruit a volunteer to come and read the story of Peter each week during this study.

Prepare

✓ Write the week's Bible verse on a markerboard or a piece of mural paper and place it where it can easily be seen: "Simon Peter said, 'You are the Christ, the Son of the Living God.'" (Matthew 16:16)

Prepare

✓ You will need the poster started two weeks ago.

Rocking the Bible Verse

• Show the children the Bible verse.

• Encourage the children to read the verse with you.

• **Say:** Now pretend you are sitting in a rocking chair. Everybody rock forward and back, forward and back.

• Encourage the children to pretend to rock.

• **Say:** Keep rocking as we read our verse again. Rock forward or back with each word.

• Lead the children in reading the verse while rocking forward and back.

Learning from Simon Peter

• Show the children the poster about learning from Peter.

• **Say:** We have been hearing stories about Simon Peter. So far we have learned that like Peter, we can follow Jesus and trust God to be with us.

• Add the following words to the poster: Believe that Jesus is God's Son.

• **Say:** Peter recognized that Jesus was the Son of God. Like Peter, we can acknowledge Jesus as God's Son. Each time we follow Jesus' teachings and example, we show that we believe Jesus is God's Son and we are his followers.

• **Ask:** What are some ways we can show that we are Jesus' followers?

• Allow children an opportunity to respond.

• **Pray:** *God, thank you for sending your Son, Jesus, to the world to show us how you want us to live. Help us find ways every day to follow Jesus and do your work. Amen.*

• Dismiss children to their small groups.

Small Groups

Divide the children into small groups. You may organize the groups around age levels or around readers and nonreaders. Keep the groups small, with a maximum of ten children in each group. You may need to have more than one group of each age level.

Younger Children

- **Say:** Like Peter, we believe Jesus is God's Son and we are followers of Jesus. As followers of Jesus, we follow Jesus' example and teachings about how to live. I am going to tell you some things about followers of Jesus. When I say something true about Jesus' followers, I want you to jump up, wave your arms in the air and say, "Yes, yes, yes! Jesus' followers do that!" If I say something that is not true, I want you to sit down, put your hands on your knees and say, "No, no, no."

- Read the following statements and encourage children to make the appropriate response.
  - o Followers of Jesus tell others about God's love. *(Yes!)*
  - o Followers of Jesus don't love anyone. *(No.)*
  - o Followers of Jesus help other people. *(Yes!)*
  - o Followers of Jesus keep God's love a secret. *(No.)*
  - o Followers of Jesus love everyone. *(Yes!)*
  - o Followers of Jesus are kind. *(Yes!)*
  - o Followers of Jesus say mean things about others. *(No.)*
  - o Followers of Jesus do good deeds. *(Yes!)*
  - o Followers of Jesus never pray. *(No.)*
  - o Followers of Jesus worship God. *(Yes!)*
  - o Followers of Jesus pray. *(Yes!)*
  - o Followers of Jesus try to avoid helping people. *(No.)*
  - o Followers of Jesus forgive other people. *(Yes!)*
  - o Followers of Jesus use hurtful words. *(No.)*
  - o Followers of Jesus encourage each other. *(Yes!)*

- **Say:** Good job! I can tell you know what it means to follow Jesus.

- **Ask:** What are some other things followers of Jesus might do? Can you tell whether someone believes Jesus is God's Son by looking at them? *(No)*

- **Say:** Followers of Jesus do not have a special color of hair or a special uniform to wear.

- **Ask:** How will people know we believe Jesus is God's Son?

- **Say:** If we are following Jesus, people will know by the way we act. The things we do and how we treat other people will show we are following Jesus.

- **Pray:** *God, like Peter, we believe in your Son, Jesus. Help us to live so that our actions show we are following Jesus. Amen.*

Prepare

✓ Provide Bibles, paper, and pencils.

Older Children

- **Say:** Today we heard Peter's story of Jesus asking the disciples who he was. Let's find this story in the Bibles.

- Have children find Matthew 16:13-20 in their Bibles.

- Read the story aloud as children follow along.

- Give each child a piece of paper.

- **Say:** Imagine that Jesus is speaking to you and asks you the question he asked the disciples that day. Think about how you would answer Jesus' question.

- Read Matthew 16:15.

- **Say:** Spend some time thinking about and writing your own response to Jesus' question. Write about who you think Jesus is and what Jesus means to you.

- Allow children time to reflect and write.

- Invite children to share their responses with the group. Remind children that sharing is always optional.

- **Pray:** *Loving God, like Peter, we acknowledge that Jesus is your Son. We want to follow Jesus. Help us find ways to follow Jesus' example of loving others and doing your work. Amen.*

Peter Recognizes Jesus as the Messiah
Based on Matthew 16:13-23

Hello! Simon Peter here again. You probably remember me telling you that I was one of Jesus' disciples. One day Jesus and I had a discussion about who he was. This was also the day that Jesus gave me the nickname Peter.

The conversation started with Jesus asking me and the other disciples what people were saying about him. It's true that people were talking about Jesus. He was attracting crowds and getting a lot of attention everywhere he went. "Who do people say I am?"

We told Jesus the things we had heard. Some people were saying he was John the Baptist come back to life. Other people thought he was Elijah. Elijah was a prophet that hadn't died but had been taken up into heaven. We'd also heard people say Jesus was Jeremiah or one of the other prophets.

Then Jesus asked us, "And what about you? Who do you say that I am?"

I had heard Jesus teach about God. I had seen him do amazing things. I knew he was God's Son, so that's what I said, "You are the Christ, the Son of the Living God."

That's when Jesus gave me the nickname of Peter. He said, "Happy are you, Simon son of Jonah, because you know this. You are Peter, which means rock, and on this rock I'll build my church."

At the time I wasn't exactly sure what Jesus meant when he said he'd build his church on me. But I truly believed Jesus was God's Son, and I was willing to follow him and do what he needed me to do.

4. Peter Denies Knowing Jesus

Objectives

The children will:

- hear the story of Peter denying Jesus.
- discover that Peter made a mistake but it is not the end of his story.
- explore ways to cope with mistakes they may make.

Bible Story

Peter Denies Knowing Jesus
Matthew 26:17-50; 69-75

Bible Verse

"I won't deny you."
(Matthew 26:35)

Focus for the Teacher

The title of this study is *Simon Peter: Flawed but Faithful Disciple*. The stories we have heard of Peter so far have mainly focused on his faithfulness. Peter answered Jesus' invitation to follow him and fish for people. Peter's faith wavered a bit when he became afraid while walking on the water, but he recognized Jesus as God's Son. Jesus gave Simon the name Peter and told him he would be the rock upon which his church was built.

Today we will hear the story of Peter making a mistake. As mistakes go, Peter's was a pretty big one. As Jesus celebrated Passover with his disciples for the last time, he told them that in the days ahead they would all deny knowing him. In response to Peter's adamant pledge that he would never deny Jesus, Jesus told Peter that Peter would deny Jesus three times before the rooster crowed. Although Peter was determined to prove Jesus wrong, he did not.

Unlike Judas, whose betrayal of Jesus was planned, Peter did not set out to deny Jesus; it just happened. After Jesus was arrested, and

> Peter's mistakes were not the end of his story.

Peter followed along at a distance. As he sat around a fire in the courtyard, the accusations began to come. "You were also with Jesus, the Galilean." "This man was with Jesus, the man from Nazareth." "You must be one of them. The way you talk gives you away."

Put yourself in Peter's place. Roman soldiers have arrested Jesus and things are starting to get ugly. Peter was scared. He may have feared that his life was in danger, and it might have been. When the accusations began, Peter acted out of self-preservation. He denied his association with Jesus. And then he heard the rooster. When the rooster crowed, Peter remembered Jesus' words. Peter had failed Jesus, even before Jesus' trial had begun. Peter cried.

Peter's mistakes were not the end of his story. Yes, Peter messed up. We all mess up at some point. Peter was not defined by his failures. Neither are we. The good news is that Peter was given another chance, and so are we.

Explore Interest Groups

Be sure that adult leaders are waiting when the first child arrives. Greet and welcome each child. Get the children involved in an activity that interests them and introduces the theme for the day's activities.

Who Is Speaking?

- Have the children sit in a circle.

- Explain the following rules to the children:
  o One child will sit in the center of the circle. That child will close his or her eyes and bow his or her head.
  o Another child will be selected by being tapped on the shoulder. That child stays in place and says, "Hello! You don't know me. I'm sure we've never met." Whoever is the speaker can attempt to disguise his or her voice.
  o The child in the center will guess who spoke. The child will have three chances to guess the speaker's identity.
  o If the speaker is correctly identified, the speaker and the guesser will change places.
  o If the speaker is not identified correctly, a new guesser will be chosen.
  o Encourage the children to play the game.

- **Say:** When we hear Peter's story today he will tell us about a time he said he didn't know somebody.

Sometimes I Feel...

- **Say:** We are going to play a game about feelings. I have some cards with feeling words on them—words that describe different emotions. One person will draw a card from the stack. Without telling or showing us the word, the person will tell us about situations or things that could result in that feeling. From the description we will try to guess the feeling.

- Invite a child to draw a card and begin the game.

- Encourage the other children to guess the emotion being described.

- Continue playing until each child has had an opportunity to describe a feeling. It is okay if a card is used more than once.

- **Say:** The story we will hear from Peter today is about a time when Peter probably felt scared and sad.

Prepare
✓ Make a copy of **Reproducible 4a: Feelings Cards**.

✓ Cut the cards apart and place them facedown in a basket.

Prepare

✓ Make copies of **Reproducible 4b: Peter's Response.**

✓ Provide pencils.

✓ Answer: "I don't know the man."

Peter's Response

- Give each child a copy of **Reproducible 4b: Peter's Response** and a pencil.

- Encourage each child to complete the puzzle.

- **Ask:** Is it true that Peter didn't know Jesus? *(No)*

- **Say:** When we hear from Peter today he will tell us why he denied knowing Jesus.

Large Group

Bring all the children together to experience the Bible story. Use a bell to alert the children to the large group time.

Show Me a Face

- Read each of the following statements and encourage the children to respond appropriately.
  - o   Show me a face you would make if you were joyful.
  - o   Show me a face you would make if you were mad.
  - o   Show me a face you would make if you were surprised.
  - o   Show me a face you would make if you were nervous.
  - o   Show me a face you would make if you were feeling guilty.
  - o   Show me a face you would make if you were scared.
  - o   Show me a face you would make if you were afraid.
  - o   Show me a face you would make if you were sad.

Simon Peter's Story

- **Say:** Today we welcome back Simon Peter to tell us another story.

- Invite your recruited volunteer to tell the story from **Reproducible 4c: Peter Denies Knowing Jesus.**

- Thank your volunteer for telling the story.

- **Ask:** Why do you think Peter said he didn't know Jesus? *(He was scared. He was afraid of being arrested too.)* How did Peter feel when he heard the rooster crow and realized he'd messed up? *(Sad, sorry, upset)*

- **Say:** Peter was in a difficult situation. Peter made a mistake. Each of us makes mistakes at some point in our life.

- **Ask:** Do you think Jesus still loved Peter even though Peter messed up? *(Absolutely!)*

- **Say:** This is not the end of the story. Peter realized he had made a mistake. He went on to tell many people about Jesus. When we realize we have made a mistake, we can also try again.

Prepare

✓ Provide copies of **Reproducible 4c: Peter Denies Knowing Jesus.**

✓ Recruit a volunteer to come and read the story of Peter each week during this study.

Prepare

✓ Write the week's Bible verse on a markerboard or a piece of mural paper and place it where it can easily be seen: "I won't deny you." (Matthew 26:35)

Emphasize the Bible Verse

- Show the children the Bible verse.

- **Ask:** Who said these words? *(Peter)*

- **Say:** We know that Peter did eventually deny knowing Jesus, but he didn't plan to deny him. It was a mistake.

- **Say:** We are going to say the Bible verse four more times. Each time we say the verse we will stress a different word. The first time we say the verse we will put the emphasis on the first word: I. The second time we say the verse we will put the emphasis on the second word: won't. We will continue until we have stressed each word in the verse.

- Encourage the children to say the Bible verse with you four times, emphasizing a different word each time.

Prepare

✓ You will need the poster started at the beginning of the study.

Learning from Simon Peter

- Show the children the poster about learning from Peter.

- **Say:** We have been hearing stories about Simon Peter. So far we have learned that like Peter, we can follow Jesus and trust God to be with us. Also like Peter, we believe Jesus is God's Son.

- Add the following words to the poster: Learn from our mistakes.

- **Say:** Today we learned about a mistake Peter made.

- **Ask:** What was Peter's mistake? *(He denied knowing Jesus.)*

- **Say:** None of us are perfect. Like Peter, we all make mistakes. Sometimes we do things that don't follow the example Jesus gave us about how God wants us to live. God didn't give up on Peter, and God doesn't give up on us either. When we make a mistake, we admit it and try to do better.

- **Pray:** *God, thank you for loving us so much that you never give up on us, even when we make mistakes. Help us to keep trying to follow Jesus' example of how you want us to live. Amen.*

- Dismiss children to their small groups.

Small Groups

Divide the children into small groups. You may organize the groups around age levels or around readers and nonreaders. Keep the groups small, with a maximum of ten children in each group. You may need to have more than one group of each age level.

Young Children

- Give each child a mirror or have the children sit where they can all look in the big mirror.
- **Say:** I am going to read some feeling words. For each word, make a face in the mirror that shows what your face might look like when you are feeling that way.
- Read the following list of feelings, allowing time for children to make each face: happy, joyful, surprised, confused, scared, lonely, angry, sad, peaceful.
- **Say:** Today we heard Peter tell us about when Jesus was arrested. Show me how you think Peter might have felt when Jesus was arrested.
- Encourage children to make faces.
- **Say:** Peter followed Jesus to the courtyard of the high priest.
- **Ask:** What happened in the courtyard? *(People accused Peter of being Jesus' friend.)*
- **Say:** Three times people said Peter had been with Jesus.
- **Ask:** What did Peter say? *(He said he didn't know Jesus.)*
- **Say:** Peter didn't know what was going to happen to Jesus. Peter might have been afraid he would get arrested too. Show me how you think Peter might have felt when people were accusing him of being Jesus' friend.
- Encourage children to make faces.
- **Say:** Then Peter heard the rooster crow. He remembered Jesus had said Peter would deny Jesus three times before the rooster crowed. Show me how you think Peter might have felt when he realized he had let Jesus down.
- Encourage children to make faces.
- **Say:** The Bible says Peter started crying.
- **Ask:** Have you ever cried? *(Of course!)*
- **Say:** It is okay to cry when we are sad or hurting. It is okay to express our feelings. Peter made a mistake and he felt bad about it.
- **Ask:** Have you ever made a mistake? *(Of course!)*
- **Say:** We all make mistakes. It happens. We do something we shouldn't or we don't do something we should. The good news is that we can try again. That's what Peter did. This is not the end of Peter's story. We will hear more from Peter next week. Peter went on to tell many people about Jesus. We can learn from Peter and not give up when we make a mistake.
- **Pray:** *God, thank you for loving us no matter what we are feeling. Thank you for loving us when we make mistakes and for helping us try again. Amen.*

Prepare
✓ Provide hand mirrors for each child or a large mirror for all children to look in.

Older Children

- **Say:** Today we heard Peter tell us about the time he denied knowing Jesus. Let's review the story.

- Encourage the children to work together to retell the story. Ask questions if necessary to help the children remember.

- **Say:** When the rooster crowed, Peter knew he had let Jesus down. He knew he had made a mistake.

- Think of a time when you promised to do something but didn't follow through. Or maybe there was a time when someone expected something from you, but you fell short of their expectations.

- **Ask:** You don't need to share the details of the situation, but how did you feel when that happened? How does it feel when you know someone is disappointed in you?

- Allow an opportunity for children to respond.

- **Say:** The good news is that this isn't the end of Peter's story. Peter didn't give up. He admitted his mistake and went on to tell many people about Jesus.

- **Ask:** Is it always easy to be a follower of Jesus and live as God wants us to live? *(No)* What do you do when you realize you have made a mistake? What makes it difficult to admit that you were wrong? What are some things you can do to correct the situation when you make a mistake?

- **Say:** When we have made a mistake it takes courage to admit that to ourselves and to other people. It takes courage to try again, knowing we could mess up again. The good news is that God is always willing to give us a second chance. Sometimes we fail to live as God wants us to. When that happens, we can admit our mistake and try again.

- **Pray:** *God, we don't always do the right thing. Like Peter, sometimes we make mistakes. Help us to recognize our mistakes and to have the courage to try again. Thank you for every time we get another chance to correct our mistakes. Amen.*

Feeling Cards

Angry	Bored	Cheerful	Confident
Confused	Curious	Disappointed	Excited
Frustrated	Giggly	Happy	Impatient
Jealous	Joyful	Lonely	Nervous
Sad	Scared	Shy	Surprised

Peter's Response

After Jesus was arrested, a woman accused Peter of being with Jesus.
To discover what Peter said, write the correct letter in each blank.

_____ You will find me twice in civic, but only once in maid.

_____ I start out donut, and finish off required.

_____ I am a vowel in olive, and also in road.

_____ You'll see me in banana, but not in bake.

_____ Look for me twice in kettle, and rattle.

_____ I'm a consonant in bake, and also in kite.

_____ I appear once in bacon, and twice in canyon.

_____ You'll find me in over, but not in very.

_____ I start out watery, and also wooden.

_____ I'm in the middle of little.

_____ You'll find me in there but not in tree.

_____ Look for me in everything but not in think or gray or vigor.

_____ I'm in middle, medium, main, and llama.

_____ I'm a vowel in always.

_____ I'm in banana but not in bake.

Peter said, "_____."

Peter Denies Knowing Jesus

Based on Matthew 26:17-50; 69-75

Hello again! Simon Peter here, back to tell you another story about the time I spent with Jesus. This is a hard story for me to tell. It is about a time I made a big mistake. As soon as I made this mistake I felt terrible. Well, let me tell you the story.

As one of Jesus' disciples, I spent a lot of time traveling with him, helping him, and learning from him. Jesus attracted a lot of attention, but not everyone liked him. Some people were angry with him. Jesus began to say some things that the other disciples and I didn't really understand. He started to talk about how he was going to be leaving us.

About three years after I became a disciple, Jesus was celebrating Passover with me and all of the other disciples. During the meal, Jesus started talking about how one of us was going to betray him. That turned out to be Judas, but we didn't know that at the time. We were confused. Then Jesus started saying we would all leave him that very night. What? There was no way I was leaving Jesus! I knew he was the Son of God. I told Jesus, "Even if everyone else leaves, I will never leave you."

I'll always remember what Jesus said to me then, "I assure you that before the rooster crows tonight, you will deny me three times." I was hurt by Jesus' words. It made me sad that he thought I would leave him.

Later that night, Jesus was arrested in a garden where he was praying. Judas led the soldiers to the garden. It was really scary. We didn't know what was going to happen to Jesus. Would those of us who were Jesus' followers be arrested too?

As Jesus had predicted, most of the disciples fled after Jesus was arrested. I followed the soldiers when they took Jesus to the house of the high priest. I waited in the courtyard to find out what would happen. While I was waiting, a servant woman said to me, "You were with Jesus too!"

I don't know what came over me. I was so frightened that I said in front of all the people there, "No! I don't know the man."

A little while later, someone else accused me of being one of Jesus' followers. "No, I'm not!" I said.

About an hour later, a third person pointed at me and said, "This man must have been with Jesus, because he is a Galilean too."

"No," I said. "I don't know what you're talking about."

Just then I heard a rooster crow. I remembered Jesus' words and realized he had been right. I had denied knowing him three times before the rooster crowed.

It still makes me sad to remember that night. It was wrong to deny knowing Jesus. I'm not proud of the mistake I made. The good news is that this wasn't the end of my story. I got another chance! I'll tell you about that next week.

5. Jesus Asks Peter a Question

Objectives

The children will:

- hear the story of Jesus asking Peter if he loved him.

- discover that Jesus told Peter to care for his followers.

- explore ways they can care for people.

Bible Story

Jesus Asks Peter a Question
John 21:1-17

Bible Verse

Jesus said to him, "Take care of my sheep."
(John 21:16b)

Focus for the Teacher

Last week we heard the story of Peter denying three times that he knew Jesus. Peter's denial of Jesus was not the end of Peter's story. Peter made a mistake when he denied Jesus. Now we will hear the story of Jesus giving Peter another chance to follow him.

Today's story takes place after Jesus' death and resurrection. It is one of the post-resurrection appearances of Jesus. This post-resurrection appearance of Jesus is not to provide evidence that he is alive. In fact, the disciples to whom Jesus appears have already seen him following his resurrection. The emphasis in this appearance story seems to be on Jesus giving directions for the future.

There are miraculous elements to this story, and a resemblance to Peter's call story that we heard in the first week of this study. The disciples have been fishing all night, but have not caught anything. In the morning they see Jesus on the shore, though they don't recognize him at first. Jesus tells them to let their net down on the other side of the boat. When Jesus' instructions are followed the result is a miraculous catch of fish—153 fish, in fact. With this miracle, Jesus is recognized. Peter is so

> The best way to show our love for Jesus is by taking care of those he loves.

excited to see Jesus that he jumps overboard and swims to shore where Jesus is, leaving the other disciples to haul in the fish.

Jesus cooks the disciples a breakfast of bread and fish. This meal is a reminder of the miraculous feeding of the five thousand with bread and fish. It is also reminiscent of Jesus' last meal with the disciples before his death when they shared the Passover meal and Jesus broke the bread.

At this point the story turns into a conversation between Jesus and Peter. Jesus asks Peter if he loves him. In fact, Jesus asks Peter this question three times, a parallel to the three times Peter denied knowing Jesus. Jesus gives Peter three opportunities to profess his love for Jesus. When Peter assures Jesus of his love, Jesus gives him directions for the future. "Feed my sheep." During his ministry, Jesus referred to himself as the good shepherd who cared for his flock—that would be us. Jesus is turning over the care of his flock to Peter. The way to show your love for me, Jesus tells Peter, is to take care of those I love. Jesus' instructions to Peter are true for us today as well. The best way to show our love for Jesus is by taking care of those he loves.

Explore Interest Groups

Be sure that adult leaders are waiting when the first child arrives. Greet and welcome each child. Get the children involved in an activity that interests them and introduces the theme for the day's activities.

Follow My Directions, Directions, Directions

- **Say:** We are going to play a game. The rules are simple. I will give you directions and you will follow them. The only other rule to the game is that you need to follow the directions that I repeat only three times. If I only say a direction once or twice, do not follow that command.

- Read the following statements and encourage the children to play the game.
  - o   Stand up. Stand up. Stand up.
  - o   Clap your hands three times. Clap your hands three times. Clap your hands three times.
  - o   Stomp your feet three times. Stomp your feet three times. Stomp your feet three times.
  - o   Snap your fingers. Snap your fingers. Snap your toes. (Some children may snap. Do not eliminate children who make a mistake.)
  - o   Pat your head. Pat your head. Pat your tummy.
  - o   Touch your toes. Touch your toes. Touch your elbows.
  - o   Shout amen. Shout amen. Shout alleluia.
  - o   Turn around. Turn around. Turn around.

- Continue playing the game using your own commands.

- Allow children to take turns giving commands of three for the other children to follow.

Prepare

✓ Provide construction paper and staplers.

✓ Use a paper cutter or scissors to cut the construction paper into nine-by-one-inch strips.

Chain of Hearts

- **Say:** Today we will hear about Jesus asking Peter whether he loved him.

- **Ask:** What symbol do we often use to represent love? (*A heart*)

- Have the children follow these directions to make a chain of paper hearts.
  - o Fold a paper strip in half bringing the short sides together.
  - o Staple the paper strip together near the folded edge.
  - o Open the paper strip and bring the two loose ends together as if you were going to fold the strip in the opposite direction.
  - o Staple the two ends together near the edges to form a heart shape.
  - o Repeat the directions to make a second heart, slipping one of the sides of the heart through the first heart before stapling the ends together.
  - o Continue adding hearts to the chain in this way.

- Encourage the children to work together to make a long paper chain of hearts.

Prepare

✓ Provide paper and pencils.

Make New Words

- Give each child a piece of paper.
- Have each child write, "Feed my sheep" at the top of the page.
- **Say:** Today we will hear about the time Jesus said these words to Peter.
- Encourage each child to make new words using only the letters in the words, Feed my sheep.
- Let the children compare their word lists.

Large Group

Bring all the children together to experience the Bible story. Use a bell to alert the children to the large group time.

Echo, Echo, Echo

- **Say:** Today we will hear Peter tell us about Jesus asking him a question. And then Jesus asks Peter the question again. Then Jesus asks Peter the question a third time. I am going to tell you the question Jesus asked Peter one word at a time. After I say each word, echo the word back to me three times.

- Read the following words to the children, pausing to let them echo each word back to you three times.
  - o   Do
  - o   you
  - o   love
  - o   me

Simon Peter's Story

- **Say:** Last week we heard about a mistake that Peter made.

- **Ask:** Do you remember what Peter's mistake was? *(He denied knowing Jesus after Jesus was arrested.)* How many times did Peter deny knowing Jesus? *(three times)*

- **Say:** Peter's mistake was not the end of his relationship with Jesus. Today Peter is going to tell us more of the story.

- Invite your recruited volunteer to tell the story from **Reproducible 5a: Jesus Asks Peter a Question**.

- Thank your volunteer for telling the story.

- **Say:** During his ministry, Jesus referred to himself as the good shepherd who took care of his flock, meaning that the people Jesus cared about were his sheep.

- **Ask:** Who are the people Jesus cares about? *(all people)*

- **Say:** When Jesus told Peter to feed his sheep, he was telling him to take care of people. That was the way that Peter could show Jesus he loved him.

Prepare

- ✓ Provide copies of **Reproducible 5a: Jesus Asks Peter a Question**.

- ✓ Recruit a volunteer to come and read the story of Peter each week during this study.

Prepare

✓ Write the week's Bible verse on a markerboard or a piece of mural paper and place it where it can easily be seen: Jesus said to him, "Take care of my sheep." (John 21:16b)

Prepare

✓ You will need the poster started at the beginning of the study.

Triple the Bible Verse

- Show the children the Bible verse.

- **Say:** This is Jesus' instructions to Peter.

- Encourage the children to read the verse with you.

- **Say:** We are going to say the Bible verse three more times. The first time we will say the verse normally. The second time we say the verse we will read each word two times. The third time we will say each word three times.

- Invite children to say the verse as directed.

Learning from Simon Peter

- Show the children the poster about learning from Peter.

- **Say:** We have been hearing stories about Simon Peter. So far we have learned that like Peter, we can follow Jesus and trust God to be with us. We also believe Jesus is God's Son. Also like Peter, we can learn from our mistakes.

- Add the following words to the poster: Care for God's people.

- **Say:** Today we heard Jesus tell Peter to take care of his sheep, or to care for God's people. Jesus' instructions for Peter are meant for us too. The best way to show we love Jesus is to show love toward other people.

- **Pray:** *God, we love you and your Son, Jesus. Help us to show that love by loving and helping others. Amen.*

- Dismiss children to their small groups.

Small Groups

Divide the children into small groups. You may organize the groups around age levels or around readers and nonreaders. Keep the groups small, with a maximum of ten children in each group. You may need to have more than one group of each age level.

Young Children

- Write the following words on a piece of paper: Jesus, Peter, fish, net, breakfast, love, and sheep. Have the children sit in a circle.

- Place the paper face down in the middle of the circle so the children cannot see the words.

- **Say:** I have written seven words from the story Peter told us today on this piece of paper. Let's see what you remember about our story. Then we'll look at the paper and see if you included all of the words.

- Have the children work together to retell today's story.

- When the children have told everything they remember, check the words to see if they have said them all. Go over anything that has been missed.

- **Ask:** What question did Jesus ask Peter three times? *(Do you love me?)* What did Jesus tell Peter to do if he loved him? *(Feed his sheep.)*

- **Say:** Jesus said that the way for Peter to show that he really loved him was for Peter to show Jesus' love to other people. Jesus would say the same thing to us. The best way to show that we love Jesus is to show love to others.

- **Ask:** Whom would Jesus want us to show love to? *(everyone, especially those in need)*

- **Say:** Let's see how many ways we can think of to "feed Jesus' sheep" or share his love.

- Show the children the stuffed sheep.

- **Say:** We are going to pass the sheep around the circle. When you are holding the sheep, tell us one way to share God's love with others. As we continue to share, try to name something that hasn't been said yet.

- Pass the sheep around the circle and encourage children to name ways to share God's love.

- **Pray:** *God, thank you for your Son, Jesus. Help us to share Jesus' love with others. Amen.*

Prepare

✓ Provide a stuffed sheep. If you do not have a stuffed sheep, use a picture of a sheep.

✓ Write the following words on a piece of paper: Jesus, Peter, fish, net, breakfast, love, and sheep.

Prepare

✓ Provide sticky notes and pencils.

✓ Identify a clear wall space to put up the sticky notes.

Older Children

- Give each child a sheet of paper and a pencil.

- **Say:** Think about the story we heard from Peter today. On your paper write down seven words you remember from our story that you think are important.

- Allow children an opportunity to write.

- Invite one child to share one word.

- **Say:** If you have also written this word, circle it on your paper.

- **Ask:** What does this word have to do with today's story?

- Continue inviting children to share their words in this way until all words have been shared and the story has been retold.

- **Ask:** What question did Jesus ask Peter three times? *(Do you love me?)* What did Jesus tell Peter to do if he loved him? *(Feed his sheep.)*

- **Say:** Jesus said that the way for Peter to show that he really loved him was for Peter to show Jesus' love to other people. Jesus would say the same thing to us. The best way to show that we love Jesus is to show love to others.

- **Ask:** Whom would Jesus want us to show love to? (everyone, especially those in need)

- **Say:** Let's see if we can think of fifty ways to "feed Jesus' sheep" or share his love.

- Allow children an opportunity to share their ideas. As the children share, record their ideas on a piece of paper.

- Have the children count to see how many ideas they have come up with.

- **Pray:** *God, thank you for your Son, Jesus. Help us to look for ways to share Jesus love with others. Amen.*

Jesus Asks Peter a Question
Based on John 21:1-17

Hello! It's Simon Peter. I'm back to tell you another story. Last week I told you about the mistake I made when I denied knowing Jesus. This week I want to tell you about how Jesus still wanted me to follow him.

You probably know that Jesus was crucified on a cross and buried. But that wasn't the end of the story! Jesus rose from the dead and appeared to me and his other followers several times before he ascended to heaven. The story I'm going to tell you is one of the times I saw Jesus after his resurrection.

One night I decided to go fishing. Six of the other disciples went with me. We fished all night but we didn't catch a single fish. In the morning, we saw a man on the shore. The man called out to us, "Have you caught anything?" When we replied that we hadn't caught a single fish, he told us to cast our nets on the right side of the boat. We did as the man said and we caught so many fish that we couldn't haul the net into the boat. We had to drag the net to shore. That's when we realized it was Jesus on the shore. I was so excited to see Jesus that I jumped overboard and swam to shore. Jesus had cooked us a breakfast of fish and bread.

After we finished eating, Jesus turned to me and asked, "Do you love me?"

I answered him, "Yes, Lord, you know I love you."

Jesus then said to me, "Feed my lambs." Then he asked me a second time, "Do you love me?"

I replied, "Yes, Lord, I do love you."

Jesus said to me, "Take care of my sheep." Then Jesus asked me a third time, "Peter, do you love me?"

"Yes," I said, "you know I love you, Lord."

Jesus said, "Then feed my sheep." Then Jesus said to me, "Follow me," just as he had when he first called me to be his disciple.

I was a little bit hurt that Jesus had asked me three times if I loved him. Didn't he know I loved him? But then I remembered I had denied knowing Jesus three times before he died. It seems appropriate that I told Jesus I loved him once for each time I denied him. I was so thankful Jesus still wanted me to be his follower.

Although Jesus told me to feed his sheep, I knew he wasn't asking me to take care of his animals. Jesus was asking me to continue the work he had started. Jesus wanted me to teach people about God, share God's love with people, and care for people. And that's what I did the rest of my life.

6. Peter Spreads the Good News

Objectives

The children will:

- hear the story of Peter telling people about Jesus.
- discover that Peter told many people about Jesus' life and teachings.
- explore ways they can spread the good news about Jesus.

Bible Story

Peter Spreads the Good News
Acts 3:1-4:22

Bible Verse

"As for us, we can't stop speaking about what we have seen and heard."

(Acts 4:20)

Focus for the Teacher

The Book of Acts tells us the stories of the early days of the church. It is the story of Jesus' followers after Jesus' resurrection and ascension to heaven. During his time on earth, Jesus prepared his followers, including Peter, to continue the work he had begun. That work was telling people about God and sharing God's love. Peter told many people about Jesus. He played an important role in the early church and helped the church to grow.

Jewish people prayed in their homes at regular times during the day. On special days, they went to the temple to pray. One afternoon Peter went to the temple to pray at the appointed time. He went with John, another disciple of Jesus. They met a man who could not walk begging outside the temple gate. Peter and John did not have money, as they had given their money to the community of believers. Instead, they restored the man's ability to walk. Peter healed the man, "in the name of Jesus Christ the Nazarene." It was important to Peter that everyone know the true source of the man's healing since there were often people present trying to perform healing in the names of other gods. When the man discovered he could walk, he entered the temple—for the first time in his life since he had been crippled since birth—and began to praise God.

When people begin to praise Peter and John for what they have done, they explain it is not by their own power that they were able to heal the man. Peter and John give the credit to God—the God who raised Jesus from the dead. For speaking of the resurrection of Jesus, Peter and John were thrown into prison. For their own reasons, the leaders in Jerusalem did not want the Jesus movement to spread.

After spending the night in prison, Peter and John are brought before Jerusalem's law court in what appears to be a sort of pre-trial hearing to determine if there is enough evidence to bring the case to trial. Ultimately, the leaders decide they cannot deny the crippled man's healing, since too many people witnessed it. Instead they ask Peter and John to stop talking about Jesus. Given a choice to obey God or obey the Jewish leaders, Peter and John chose to continue to do God's work, assisted and inspired by the Holy Spirit. Peter continued to spread the good news about Jesus for the rest of his life.

> Peter told many people about Jesus.

Explore Interest Groups

Be sure that adult leaders are waiting when the first child arrives. Greet and welcome each child. Get the children involved in an activity that interests them and introduces the theme for the day's activities.

Good News Tag

- **Say:** We have been learning about Peter. Jesus called Peter to fish for people. Even after Jesus' death and resurrection, Peter continued to tell people about Jesus. Peter told people the good news that God loves them. We are going to play a game of tag to remind us of the good news Peter told people about. If you are tagged, you must sit down and stay in one spot until someone says, "Good news, (name), God loves you!" They must use your name in order to unfreeze you. As you are playing, remember to look for friends that may need your help to rejoin the game.

- Choose a child to be the first tagger. If you have a large class, choose more than one child to be tagger.

- Encourage children to play the game.

Prepare

- ✓ Identify a large, open area free of obstacles to play the game.

Leaping Letters

- Give each child a copy of **Reproducible 6a: Leaping Letters** and a pencil.

- Encourage each child to solve the puzzle.

- Have children check their answers by looking up Acts 4:20 in their Bibles.

Prepare

- ✓ Make copies of **Reproducible 6a: Leaping Letters** for each child.

- ✓ Provide Bibles and pencils.

- ✓ *Answer:* As for us, we can't stop speaking about what we have seen and heard.

Prepare

✓ Provide a CD player and a CD of upbeat Christian children's music.

✓ Set up a circle of chairs facing the chairs to the outside of the circle, using one less chair than the number of children playing.

Musical Review Game

- Have the children form a circle around the chairs.

- Start playing music and have the children begin walking around the circle.

- **Say:** When the music stops, find a chair.

- Stop the music and have each child find a seat.

- **Say:** You are not out of the game if you are left standing. Rather, you will tell us something that you remember about Peter.

- Invite the child left standing to share something they remember.

- Remove a chair and start playing the music again, having the children walk around the circle.

- Stop the music and have each child find a seat. This time two people will be left standing.

- Invite each standing child to share something they remember about Peter. Encourage them to think of things that have not been shared already.

- Continue playing the game, removing one additional chair each round.

Large Group

Bring all the children together to experience the Bible story. Use a bell to alert the children to the large group time.

Praise God

- **Say:** It is always good to take time to praise God. There are many ways to praise God. I am going to tell you a way to praise God. Continue doing each action until I call out another way to praise God. Be aware of other people so you don't run into each other. As you praise God with your body, thank God for the ability to move.

- Give the children the following instructions, allowing a time for them to follow each instruction before moving on to the next one:
  o Praise God by leaping for joy!
  o Praise God by marching!
  o Praise God by stomping your feet!
  o Praise God by clapping!
  o Praise God by hopping on one foot!
  o Praise God by placing your hands on your hips and twisting side to side!
  o Praise God by waving your arms overhead!
  o Praise God by jumping up and down!
  o Praise God by sitting down!

Simon Peter's Story

- Provide copies of **Reproducible 6b: Peter Spreads the Good News.**

- Recruit a volunteer to come and read the story of Peter each week during this study.

- **Say:** We have been learning about Simon Peter. Today we will hear one more story from Peter.

- Invite your recruited volunteer to tell the story from **Reproducible 6b: Peter Spreads the Good News.**

- Thank your volunteer for telling the story.

- **Ask:** What did the council of leaders ask Peter and John to do? *(stop talking about Jesus)*

- **Say:** The leaders were worried about the followers of Jesus growing in number. They were afraid they would lose their power. But Peter and John knew that God's authority is greater than the authority of any men. Peter and John chose to obey God and to continue spreading the good news about Jesus. Peter continued to tell people about Jesus for the rest of his life.

Prepare

✓ Provide copies of **Reproducible 6b: Peter Spreads the Good News.**

✓ Recruit a volunteer to come and read the story of Peter each week during this study.

Prepare

✓ Write the week's Bible verse on a markerboard or a piece of mural paper and place it where it can easily be seen: "As for us, we can't stop speaking about what we have seen and heard." (Acts 4:20)

Prepare

✓ You will need the poster started at the beginning of the study.

Spread the Bible Verse

- Show the children the Bible verse.

- **Say:** This was Peter and John's response when they were told to stop telling people about Jesus.

- Encourage the children to read the verse with you.

- **Say:** When Peter and John told people about Jesus they were spreading the good news. Today we are going to spread the Bible verse

- Choose two children in the middle of the room to begin the Bible verse.

- **Say:** (Children's names) are going to read the Bible verse. Then they will say the verse again and anyone who is sitting next to or directly in front of or directly behind them will join in and say the verse too. We will keep repeating the verse over and over. When the person next to you or in front of you or behind you says the verse, then the next time you will join in with us.

- Begin saying the verse and continue repeating it until everyone is saying the verse together.

Learning From Simon Peter

- Show the children the poster about learning from Peter.

- **Say:** We have been hearing stories about Simon Peter. So far we have learned that like Peter, we can follow Jesus and trust God to be with us. We believe Jesus is God's Son. We learn from our mistakes. Also like Peter, we care for God's people.

- Add the following words to the poster: Spread the good news.

- **Say:** Peter helped spread the good news about Jesus. He helped start the early church. Jesus was right when he said he would build his church upon Peter the Rock. Think about a time you received some really great news – a time you learned something really exciting.

- **Ask:** When you have great news do you want to keep it to yourself, or do you want to tell someone about it?

- **Say:** Peter couldn't keep the good news about Jesus to himself. Good news is meant to be shared. We can tell people about Jesus like Peter did.

- **Pray:** *God, thank you for loving us and thank you for sending your Son, Jesus, to teach us about you. Help us to remember to look for ways to tell people about your love. Amen.*

- Dismiss children to their small groups

Small Groups

Divide the children into small groups. You may organize the groups around age levels or around readers and nonreaders. Keep the groups small, with a maximum of ten children in each group. You may need to have more than one group of each age level.

Young Children

- **Say:** We have learned a lot about Peter these six weeks. After Jesus' death and resurrection, Peter continued Jesus' ministry. Peter was important in helping the church grow. He told many people about Jesus.

- **Ask:** Do you remember how you learned about Jesus?

- **Say:** You know about Jesus because somebody, and probably more than one person, has shared this good news with you. It is important that we tell people about Jesus. One way we can share the good news about Jesus is to invite someone to church or Sunday school. Think about someone you know that you might invite to come to church with you some Sunday. Maybe it's someone you know that doesn't go to church, or someone who has recently moved to town. Don't say the person's name out loud, but just think of someone in your mind.

- Give the children a few moments to think of someone they could invite.

- **Ask:** What are some things you could tell this person that would make them not want to come to church with you?

- Give the children an opportunity to share their bad ideas of how to invite someone to church. Encourage children to share their silly ideas. Allowing the children to share goofy ideas will help them feel comfortable sharing.

- **Ask:** Now that we know what not to do, what are some things you could say to invite this person to church with you that might make them want to come to church with you?

- Give the children an opportunity to share their good ideas of how to invite someone to church.

- **Say:** We have come up with some very good ideas. I encourage you to use those ideas to invite someone you know to come to church with you.

- **Pray:** *God, thank you for opportunities to learn about Peter. Help us to find ways to be like Peter and tell people about your love and about your Son, Jesus. Amen.*

Prepare

✓ Provide sticky notes and pencils.

✓ Identify a clear wall space to put up the sticky notes.

Older Children

- **Say:** We have learned a lot about Peter over the last six weeks. After Jesus' death and resurrection, Peter continued Jesus' ministry. Peter was important in helping the church grow. He told many people about Jesus. As followers of Jesus, telling people about Jesus is one of our jobs. We can be like Peter and tell people about Jesus.

- **Ask:** Is it possible to tell people about Jesus without using words? How can you share the good news about Jesus without saying anything?

- Allow children an opportunity to share their thoughts and ideas.

- **Say:** Anytime you share God's love with someone or help someone or act with kindness, you are sharing the good news. Showing people love is one of the best ways to spread the news of God's love.

- Give each child a pad of sticky notes.

- **Say:** We are going to brainstorm ways to share the good news without saying a word. Think of ways to share the good news with your actions. Write each idea on a separate sticky note and put it up on the wall. I am going to give you three minutes. Keep coming up with ideas until I tell you to stop. Let's see how many ideas you can come up with. Remember we aren't using words, so we will do this quietly.

- Encourage the children to write ideas on sticky notes and put them on the wall.

- After three minutes, **Say:** You came up with a lot of ideas. Let's take a look.

- Invite the children to silently read the ideas others have written and posted on the wall.

- **Say:** As you consider all the ideas we came up with, think about which ideas you could do in the upcoming week. Choose two or three sticky notes and take them home with you to remind you to share the good news without using words this week. You can choose ideas other than the ones you wrote.

- Invite each child to take two or three sticky notes home.

- **Say:** We can be like Peter and help spread the good news with our words and our actions.

- **Pray:** *God, thank you for an opportunity to learn about Peter. Help us to use what we have learned to be better followers of Jesus. Help us to share your love with everyone we meet. Amen.*

Leaping Letters

Peter and another disciple of Jesus healed a man who had been crippled since birth. When the man discovered he could walk he was so happy he began leaping for joy. Peter told everyone that they healed the man in Jesus' name. The leaders of the town wanted Peter and John to stop talking about Jesus. Solve the puzzle to discover Peter and John's response to this request.

The letters in the sentence below have taken a leap. Each letter has jumped to the next letter in the alphabet. To decode the message, write the correct letters on the lines provided

B T   G P S   V T '   X F

D B O   U   T U P Q

T Q F B L J O H   B C P V U

X I B U   X F   I B W F

T F F O   B O E   I F B S E .

Peter Spreads the Good News

Based on Acts 3:1–4:22

Hello, Simon Peter here! I'm back to tell you one more story. Today I am going to tell you about something that happened after Jesus' resurrection and after Jesus had returned to heaven. It was hard for those of us that followed Jesus not to have him with us on earth anymore. Before Jesus left, he told us we were to continue doing the ministry he had started. We had a job to do. We were to tell people about Jesus and the things that Jesus taught about. So that's what we did.

One day I was going to the temple to pray. I was with my friend John, another disciple of Jesus. Outside of the temple we met a man who had been crippled since birth. The man was begging for money. John and I didn't have any money, but we did have the power of the Holy Spirit. We healed the man and he was able to walk again. The man leaped up and went into the temple, praising God as he went.

When people saw that the man was healed, they began praising John and me. I made sure people knew that we had healed the man in Jesus' name. I began to preach and tell people about Jesus. The temple guards didn't like people preaching about Jesus, so they threw John and me into prison.

The next day we were brought before a council of leaders and legal experts. They began to question us about how we had healed the man. I began to preach again. I told the council about Jesus.

The council finally decided they couldn't keep us in prison for healing someone. They decided to let us go, but they warned us that we should stop talking about Jesus. They didn't want the news about Jesus to spread.

Stop talking about Jesus? There was no way John and I were willing to do that. I told the council, "We can't stop speaking about what we have seen and heard." And I didn't stop speaking about Jesus. I kept telling people about Jesus. I told people about Jesus' life and ministry and the things he had taught us about God. I spent the rest of my life telling people about Jesus.

CPSIA information can be obtained
at www.ICGtesting.com
Printed in the USA
LVHW102042091118
596595LV00003B/18/P